Musical Instruments

Violin

By Nick Rebman

www.littlebluehousebooks.com

Copyright © 2023 by Little Blue House, Mendota Heights, MN 55120. All rights reserved. No part of this book may be reproduced or utilized in any form or by any means without written permission from the publisher.

Little Blue House is distributed by North Star Editions:
sales@northstareditions.com | 888-417-0195

Produced for Little Blue House by Red Line Editorial.

Photographs ©: Shutterstock Images, cover, 4, 7, 9, 11, 13, 14–15, 17, 19, 21, 23, 24 (top left), 24 (top right), 24 (bottom left), 24 (bottom right)

Library of Congress Control Number: 2022911131

ISBN
978-1-64619-704-0 (hardcover)
978-1-64619-736-1 (paperback)
978-1-64619-797-2 (ebook pdf)
978-1-64619-768-2 (hosted ebook)

Printed in the United States of America
Mankato, MN
012023

About the Author

Nick Rebman is a writer and editor who lives in Minnesota. He enjoys reading, walking his dog, and playing rock songs on his drum set.

Table of Contents

My Violin **5**

Glossary **24**

Index **24**

My Violin

I play the violin.

It sounds nice.

I play the violin.

It has four strings.

I play the violin.

I hold the bow in my right hand.

I play the violin.

I move the bow across the strings.

I play the violin.

I press the strings with my left hand.

I play the violin.

I have a teacher.

I play the violin.

I learn to read sheet music.

I play the violin.

I practice in my room.

I play the violin.

I get better and better.

I play the violin.

I am in a band.

Glossary

band

sheet music

bow

teacher

Index

B
bow, 8, 10

H
hand, 8, 12

S
strings, 6, 10, 12

T
teacher, 14